Ethan Hunt

For His Glory

Using our written words to
have the greatest impact on
the world around us.

Christ Is Risen Ministries

FOR HIS GLORY

ISBN 978-1542805858

FOR HIS GLORY: USING OUR WRITTEN WORDS TO HAVE THE GREATEST IMPACT ON THE WORLD AROUND US/ETHAN HUNT -1ST EDITION

1.CHRISTIANITY 2. WRITING 3.MOTIVATION

PRINTED IN THE UNITED STATES OF AMERICA 2017

THECAGELESSMOVEMENT.COM

CONTENTS:

DON'T STOP WHEN YOU'RE

TIRED. STOP WHEN YOU'RE DONE!

DREAM BIG

In order to be successful in accomplishing your finished book, you must first realize and believe that all things are possible with God! There is not a thing that is too big for Him! You must really believe that in your heart! Secondly, you must come to the realization that He does not make mistakes and that He made you for a very specific purpose here on earth. Let everything you do glorify Him! If you're writing this book to glorify Him you will not fail! Three things got me to the finish line with my books; passion, perseverance, and faith. These three things are critical in finishing your project! Most of all, surrender all will and emotion to the Lord. Let His will be done through you. You can't do a thing under your own will because it will draw you away from God. Be free and light in His will for your life and you won't go wrong!

This book is meant to be a tool so I am providing extra pages for you to write your personal notes in. Don't be afraid to scribble down your thoughts and feelings as you go along.

Before you begin, set some personal time apart to seek the Lord. Clear your mind and let Him tell you what He has planned for you to write about.

Do You Believe That Your Book Will Change the World?

_____

_____

_____

_____

_____

_____

_____

_____

_____

_____

_____

_____

_____

_____

_____

_____

_____

_____

_____

"HOW WONDERFUL IT IS
THAT NOBODY NEED WAIT
A SINGLE MOMENT
BEFORE STARTING TO
IMPROVE THE WORLD." -
ANNE FRANK

Title Choice

First of all, you're going to want to pick a title that's both unique and catchy. Don't settle for less because your name is behind your title. It may seem like a small thing to consider but it's the first step in producing a book and it's where you'll draw your passion and inspiration from as you type. It's going to represent you and your project to the public so make sure to put a lot of emphasis on it! Make good choices!

Brainstorm Possible Title Names.

_____

_____

_____

_____

_____

_____

_____

_____

_____

_____

_____

_____

_____

_____

_____

_____

_____

_____

_____

_____

_____

_____

_____

_____

_____

"ONLY PUT OFF UNTIL TOMMORROW WHAT YOU ARE WILLING TO DIE HAVING LEFT UNDONE" -PICASSO

Contents

Another main thing that pulls your project together is your contents. Some authors choose not to publish a page of contents but even if you choose not to it is still beneficial to have them to collect your thoughts. I always have my contents written down as kind of a road map at the beginning of each of my books. This way I'm not confused along the way but have a clear path to guide me along the book's journey. Let the Lord give you chapter by chapter. He's a God of order so He knows exactly what He's doing! Surrender to His plans for your book. Often with my writing, He'll give me a certain memory about something He wants me to write about.

Get Organized. Write Your Chapters in Order.

_____

_____

_____

_____

_____

_____

_____

_____

_____

_____

_____

_____

_____

_____

_____

_____

_____

_____

_____

_____

_____

_____

_____

"YOU DON'T HAVE TO SEE THE WHOLE STAIRCASE, JUST TAKE THE FIRST STEP." -MARTIN LUTHER KING JR

Header & Page

I find that adding a header to the top of the page really helps the book to be more professional in its appearance and adds value to its authenticity! You can do this in most typing programs by clicking the insert tab and clicking on the header button. Also on the insert tab you'll find, "Insert page number." Here you can add page numbers to your book and format them to start and stop wherever you'd prefer them in your manuscript. At the end of every chapter insert a "page break" by clicking on the insert tab. Also, if you need to add a chapter between chapters click on "insert page" on the insert tab. I'd recommend maybe taking a course on Microsoft Word, a typing class, and some English. It's not completely required but it will speed up the writing processes for your each of your books. As a student taking these classes, I believed they were completely useless, boy was I wrong!

What Challenges Do You See With This Book?

_____

_____

_____

_____

_____

_____

_____

_____

_____

_____

_____

_____

_____

_____

_____

_____

_____

_____

_____

_____

_____

_____

_____

"WHEN THERE IS A HILL TO CLIMB, DON'T THINK THAT WAITING WILL MAKE IT SMALLER." - UNKNOWN

Chapter Structure

Begin your first chapter by adding a title chapter. I like to play with different fonts to match the personality of my books. It's good to be unique and out of the box while yet staying within the lines of professionalism. You want to make this book yours. I tend to have an opening phrase in a different font than my title font to add texture to my pages and take my reader smoothly into each of my chapters. Each chapter should correlate and add another piece of useful information to your book's story. Throughout writing your book, you can use your first chapter as a reference to look back on throughout your project. If you need a visual, feel free to flip through any of my books as you write yours!

What Will Be The Message Behind Your Book?

_____

_____

_____

_____

_____

_____

_____

_____

_____

_____

_____

_____

_____

_____

_____

_____

_____

_____

_____

_____

_____

_____

_____

_____

"THINGS MAY COME TO THOSE WHO WAIT, BUT ONLY THE THINGS LEFT BY THOSE WHO HUSTLE." -ABRAHAM LINCOLN

SET A GOAL

It's essential to write down and speak out a goal to have your book done by. No matter what, do not stray from this goal, keep at it till your victorious! The enemy will bring about mysterious circumstances to stall your progress so you need to pray and rest in the peace of God. He can protect you from the snares of the devil!

Set A Goal. When Will Your Book Be Done By? Don't Make Excuses.

_____

_____

_____

_____

_____

_____

_____

_____

_____

_____

_____

_____

_____

_____

_____

_____

_____

_____

_____

_____

_____

_____

"BEGIN TO WEAVE AND GOD WILL GIVE YOU THE THREAD"- GERMAN PROVERB

Passion

After the success of my first book, I've had numerous people ask me to teach and help them write their own books. To be truthful, it was a little overwhelming so that's how the concept for this book was born. I believe the Lord has given me the idea for this guide so that I can help people realize their own potential to make an impact on the communities around them.

A big part of writing a book is passion! Personal passion. You're the only one with the actual memories and emotions of the events you'll write about so it is important that it is you who is pouring your own personal passion into your book! Passion is the energy that keeps the words flowing from your memories. It is only you that can tap into that raw power!

List Some Key Take Aways You Want Your Reader To Learn.

_____

_____

_____

_____

_____

_____

_____

_____

_____

_____

_____

_____

_____

_____

_____

_____

_____

_____

_____

_____

_____

_____

_____

"FOLLOWING THROUGH IS THE ONLY THING THAT SEPARATES DREAMERS FROM PEOPLE THAT ACCOMPLISH GREAT THINGS"-GENE HAYDEN

Perseverance

Another important element of writing is perseverance. Unless you continuously move forward daily on your book, it won't get nowhere. Procrastination can be your single worst obstacle in finishing. Sometimes it may feel hard, or you may feel too tired but you can't take "no" for an answer. Think back to the last time you worked out. Physically, you probably had to fight yourself tooth and nail to start and finish. Like exercise, even when it hurts, you must push through. Remember your doing this for the King! You have the potential to reach and change millions of people's hearts towards their Savior. This could be the single most important thing you ever accomplish in life! Never give an excuse, just do it and soon it will flow naturally with your lifestyle until you have finally reached your goal!

How Bad Do You Really Want This? Push Hard!

_____

_____

_____

_____

_____

_____

_____

_____

_____

_____

_____

_____

_____

_____

_____

_____

_____

_____

_____

_____

_____

_____

_____

_____

_____

"A YEAR FROM NOW YOU MAY WISH YOU HAD STARTED TODAY"- KAREN LAMB

Faith

Lastly, and most importantly comes faith. You must trust in God and you need to believe in yourself that you can accomplish what He's put in your heart to do. Imagine once you make it to Heaven and see all the lives you've impacted here on earth! It's going to be so worth it! The thought of this should excite you to make it till the end. Don't get discouraged when people may mock you or tell you that you can't do it. You can do anything because God is with you!

List How Faithful The Lord Has Been In Your Life.

_____

_____

_____

_____

_____

_____

_____

_____

_____

_____

_____

_____

_____

_____

_____

_____

_____

_____

_____

_____

_____

_____

_____

"HOW SOON 'NOT NOW' BECOMES 'NEVER'"- MARTIN LUTHER

Final Instructions

This book can either be a peaceful, healing process, or a rough, stressful process. Operate under the power of God's peace and don't let the enemy bully you. This is going to be a lot of hard work and take a lot of dedication. It might be one of the hardest things you ever undertake! But know that if God called you to this mission, no force of hell will be able to stop you! If I can do it, then so can you!

Lord God, in the name of Your Son, Jesus, my brothers and sisters and I boldly approach Your throne. You said in Your Word, anything we agree on You will do and if we ask and believe we will receive. We thank You for all You have done to get us to this point in our lives. I ask that You bless my readers with the gifting's, abilities and talents to accomplish their books with passion, perseverance and faith. We write all our works to glorify You! Bring Your Kingdom to earth and snatch Your children from the claws of the enemy! Thank You in advance for what You're about to do through my reader's projects. Amen.

I believe it's extremely important to hold yourself accountable to your hopes and dreams. When it comes down to it, it's not everyone else that can stop you from accomplishing your destiny, but yourself. To commit to finishing this project that the Lord has placed on your heart, please write the name of your title, your signature and date, promising yourself that you will finish what you started no matter what!

Title:_____

Signature:_____

Date:_____

"WHATEVER YOU **DO**, **WORK** AT IT WITH **ALL** YOUR **HEART**, AS

WORKING FOR THE **LORD**, NOT FOR MEN."- THE APOSTLE PAUL

Notes

_____

_____

_____

_____

_____

_____

_____

_____

_____

_____

_____

_____

_____

_____

_____

_____

_____

_____

_____

_____

_____

_____

_____

_____

_____

_____

_____

_____

_____

_____

_____

_____

_____

_____

_____

_____

_____

_____

_____

_____

_____

_____

_____

_____

_____

_____

_____

_____

_____

_____

_____

_____

_____

_____

_____

_____

_____

_____

_____

_____

_____

_____

_____

_____

_____

_____

_____

_____

_____

_____

_____

_____

_____

_____

_____

_____

_____

_____

_____

_____

_____

_____

_____

_____

_____

_____

_____

_____

_____

_____

_____

_____

_____

_____

_____

_____

_____

_____

_____

_____

_____

_____

_____

_____

_____

_____

_____

_____

_____

_____

_____

_____

_____

_____

_____

_____

_____

_____

_____

_____

_____

_____

_____

_____

_____

_____

_____

_____

_____

_____

_____

_____

_____

_____

_____

_____

_____

_____

_____

_____

Writing Lessons

If you'd like to hire Ethan to personally help you write your own book please sign up on his website, thecagelessmovement.com